Scripture quotations are from the King James Version of the Holy Bible unless otherwise indicated.

ISBN: 978-1-7333167-2-9

Published by: Royalty Kingdom Publishing

ROYALTY KINGDOM
PUBLISHING

Edited by:
Sharlyne Thomas
Spirit of Excellence Writing & Editing Services, LLC
www.TakeUpThySword.com

Introduction

First, let me begin by saying, I believe by faith that whatever your reasons are for seeking a fasting study guide, God will honor your faithfulness to your fast. I am encouraged by your desire to grow, and your belief and understanding of God's Word. I believe fasting is crucial for our spiritual growth. Fasting creates a spiritual climate or environment that allows us to eliminate distractions and focus on the Word and the voice of God.

I have fasted many times for many different lengths of time and for many different things. Over the past 3 years, I have participated in an annual 40-day fast. The last 2 years, I had the honor of facilitating the fast, which meant that I had to prepare the daily devotional for the entire group for the entire 40 days. That experience was equally challenging and amazing. God began to reveal His Word to me so clearly and vividly that it seemed effortless to write the devotionals. He also prepared me and gave me discernment about attacks to come as a result of our decision to fast.

The participants of the fast consisted of close friends and family. As a result of our faithfulness, God answered prayers and moved in a mighty way. A short time following the conclusion of our fast, my loving and supportive husband suggested that I create a 40-day fasting guide and so, here it is. The purpose of this fasting workbook is to prompt you to investigate yourself on a spiritual level. I aim to challenge you during this 40-day journey so you can stretch and grow, increasing your faith, achieving your dreams and ultimately, strengthening and edifying the Body of Christ.

What you will need: You will need a Bible and a willing and committed heart. I recommend an online version to reference various translations of the Bible. May God bless, strengthen and keep you as you commence your 40-day journey.

Why Do We Fast?

In Matthew 16:24, Jesus tells us that to be able to follow Him, we have to deny ourselves and take up our cross. Romans 8:7 says that a carnal mind is enmity against God so for us to begin to follow Christ, we have to begin by crucifying or denying our flesh. Our flesh does not want us to grow closer with God, to mature and develop our spirit man. I believe that the act fasting can propel us to a higher level in Christ. Denying the flesh rebels and represses the carnal man, which provides an opportunity for the spirit man to mature, strengthen and grow in Christ.

There are numerous benefits to fasting. Immediately, the correlation between fasting and prayer produces increased communication with God. The act of fasting itself promotes a sharpened connection with God by removing hindering distractions and allowing a clear, uninhibited mind to communicate with God. Without inhibition or obstruction, there is now a clear and direct path to seek God and His Word with a purposeful focus. Understanding why you are fasting is of the utmost importance. You must know your purpose or reason for fasting. Keeping your purpose in mind will help to guide you as you continue to pray throughout your fast.

Often, the Bible shows fasting as a means to receive a specific request from God. It is imperative to recognize that God is still God and our request must be within His will. He knows and wants what is best for us. At times, the understanding of God and who He is can be misconstrued, causing us to believe that whatever is asked of God, He will do it. God is not a genie and our wishes are not His command. God has established basic principles: what you sow, you will reap and as you give, it will be given back to you. Those fundamental truths still apply. Be cognizant and deliberate about what you are fasting for, ensuring that your request is in line with the Will of God.

In the Bible, there are multiple examples of fasting, as well as instructions on how to fast. In Ezra 8:21-23, Ezra is fasting for traveling mercies and protection for his journey to Jerusalem.

3

Second Samuel, chapter 12, shows King David fasting for the life of his son. In this passage, it is important to note that the loss of David's son was a direct result of his decision to have Uriah killed so he could marry Bathsheba. David fasted with the hope of God allowing the child to live. Unfortunately for David, despite his fasting, it was not God's will for the child to live. Keep in mind that fasting does not override God's principle stated in Galatians 6:7 that "whatsoever a man soweth, that shall he also reap." For every action, there is a reaction; for every cause, there is an effect. Acts 13:1-3 gives a example of fasting for direction. While Barnabas and Saul were worshipping, praying and fasting, the Holy Spirit gave them instruction to go do "the work whereunto I have called them."

My personal experience with fasting is that it allows me to block out distractions and I am able to concentrate solely on God. I have a greater understanding of His Word and I am able to hear clearly from the Lord. Consider someone with poor vision wearing glasses for the first time or turning on the defrost after the front windshield has fogged up: everything is clear and in focus. I have found that during a fast, I am extremely organized and productive. Fasting provides me with clarity unlike at any other time. Although fasting is a tremendous sacrifice for me, especially because I truly enjoy eating, it has always been a tremendous blessing. I pray that you too will be blessed by your fasting experience, and that you will make it a regular part of your lifestyle.

How Do We Fast?

There are multiple ways to fast. All throughout the Bible you can find different people fasting different things for different amounts of time and for different reasons. You can fast alone or with a group; although ultimately, fasting is a personal journey between you and God. Fasting can be done for multiple hours or multiple days; you can fast a type of food group or something as specific as TV or Facebook.

Here are a few examples of people who fasted in the Bible: In Esther 4:16, Esther asked the Hebrew people to go on a fast for three days with no food or drink when she needed to approach the king to save her people from Haman's plot. Second Samuel 12:16-20 says that David fasted until the seventh day when his son died, and then he worshipped and ate. The first chapter of Daniel describes a 10-day fast of no meat or wine. Daniel also fasted again in the tenth chapter for 21 days with no bread, meat or wine.

If we look at 1 Corinthians 7:5, we see that as Paul was explaining the principles of marriage, he mentioned that while fasting, married couples can refrain from sex with consent for a time to completely commit to fasting and prayer. This shows us that we can fast from things other than food. We must remember that fasting should not be easy; if you can go all day without eating, fasting from food may not be the best option for you. Fasting should cause your flesh to be unhappy; crucifying your flesh should not feel good or be comfortable. I love to eat, so fasting food is a logical choice for me. If you spend hours playing video games, reading or watching TV, then fasting from those things may be a better alternative to free your mind and create more opportunity for prayer.

The first step after deciding to fast is to determine why you are fasting. You may be fasting for multiple reasons and that is perfectly fine. Narrowing your request will allow a directed focus on what you are praying about.

Next, it is imperative to set realistic parameters for your fast, detailing the amount of time you are fasting. You can fast for a specific amount of hours in a day or possibly days in a month. You may want to fast certain meals per day, particular foods, objects or activities. Your parameters include:

1. Why have you decided to fast?

_____

2. What are you fasting from?

_____

3. What is the duration of your fast?

_____

NOTE: If you are a diabetic, it may not be wise for you to attempt to fast all day.

One of the keys to a successful fast is being realistic with your expectation of yourself. Planning a 40-day fast with no food or water for your first fast may be a bit impractical. Plan for something difficult but not so much that you end up breaking your fast. Honoring your commitment to the fast is just as important as fasting itself. God has always been faithful to His Word, so we should be faithful to ours. In Judges, chapter 11, there is a story about a man named Jephthah who teaches us to be careful what we say and also to commit once you have made your vow regardless of the consequence. This man made a vow to God that he may not have thought out completely, and it ultimately cost him his daughter's life. Be prudent when establishing your parameters so you will be able to follow through with them.

Once you have set your parameters, choose a start date. Allow time to prepare your mind, heart and any materials or meals you may need to plan for by shopping or meal prepping for the upcoming week. When you are ready to start your fast, begin with the expectation to receive what you are asking for. James 1:6-8 (NKJV) says that a man who doubts should not expect to receive anything from the Lord. Finally, completely commit. Do not cheat (this is why realistic goals are important); do what you said you would do. If you do your part, God will do His.

Steps to Fasting

1. Establish your reasons for fasting.
2. Set realistic parameters to follow.
3. Choose a start date, allowing mental and physical prep time.
4. Begin with an expectation to receive what you are asking for; eliminate all doubt.
5. Completely commit.

Suggestions: I have found that keeping a journal is helpful when fasting. Writing down how you feel and documenting your spiritual encounters can prove valuable when witnessing to someone or as a reminder of past victories. Recording your spiritual experiences is useful when God's promises begin to manifest. To be able to look back and see exactly what God said and what He did is amazing. In Isaiah 48:5-8, God is telling the children of Israel that He always tells us what is to come; God always speaks. It is wise to document what God says so you always have a log or diary to reference and see what God has done.

Also, you may consider fasting with a partner or a group. Group fasts are beneficial for those times when you are struggling with your commitment and may need some support. I have been in situations where I was weak and wanted to break the fast for some reason or another, but one of the other people fasting encouraged me enough to withstand that particular temptation. Matthew 18:19 says that when we come together in agreement, God will grant our request. First Thessalonians 5:11 (NCV) instructs us to encourage each other and give each other strength. I feel that fasting within a group creates a common bond and brings the participants of the group closer together.

Function of This Study Guide

What you will find in this study guide:

- *Daily Prayer* - To encourage and remind you to keep open the lines of communication between you and God.

- *Daily Scripture* - To encourage you to seek a deeper understanding of God. Drawing closer to Christ requires knowing who He is through His Word. The Bible is the living Word, so I pray that the scripture will prompt you to study His Word more extensively. I also pray that the scripture will offer a different perspective or prompt you to search a comprehensive or well-rounded and complete understanding of the Word.

- *Discussion* - These discussions intend to connect the application of the scripture to your everyday life and aim to challenge you to either apply it to your life or examine a previous situation that you can relate the scripture to.

- *Reflections* - This is where you have the opportunity to share your thoughts and experiences concerning the fast. You can write about how difficult or not so difficult the fast is and any adjustments you may have to make. You can share how the scriptures were helpful and how they were applied to your life. This is also a place for you to record your communication encounters with Christ. Going back to see how God spoke to you through a scripture, song, person, the preached Word or a prophet can be helpful when you are feeling low or going through a tough time. It may be necessary to go back and remember past victories and past communication so you can be encouraged that if God brought you through that situation, He can bring you through anything.

- *Weekly Challenge* - At the beginning of the week, you will be challenged to improve in a specific area pertaining to a topic discussed during that week. You can express how well you were able to complete your challenge, and record and examine the reasons you felt the challenge was simple or difficult for you.

- *Prayer Request Log* - On your prayer request log, you will be able to record your prayer request, the date, the answer to your prayer request and the date it was answered. Keeping a log will establish a foundation of trust, giving you an opportunity to exercise your faith and encourage you during future times of struggle. At times, we tend to allow our situations and circumstances to appear greater than our God. Your prayer log will act as a reference to remind you that God delivered you before and He can surely do it again.

Prayer Requests

Date   **Prayer Request**

___   _____

___   _____

___   _____

___   _____

___   _____

___   _____

___   _____

___   _____

___   _____

___   _____

___   _____

___   _____

___   _____

Answered Prayer Log

Date   **How God Answered Your Prayer**

——   ———————————————————————

——   ———————————————————————

——   ———————————————————————

——   ———————————————————————

——   ———————————————————————

——   ———————————————————————

——   ———————————————————————

——   ———————————————————————

——   ———————————————————————

——   ———————————————————————

——   ———————————————————————

——   ———————————————————————

——   ———————————————————————

——   ———————————————————————

Day 1

Daily Prayer: *Heavenly Father, I thank You for another day and this 40-day fasting journey. I pray, oh God, that You will open my heart, my mind and my ears so that I can receive all that You have for me. Lord, I pray that through this fast, I will draw closer to You, gain a deeper understanding of Your plan for my life, experience You in a way I never have before, and grow and develop into a stronger and more mature witness for You. I love You, Lord; thank You for loving me, in Jesus' name, Amen.*

Ask and you shall receive-**Daily Scriptures:** Matthew 21:22-24, Matthew 7:7

Discussion: As you begin this fasting journey, I want to encourage you to ask God for whatever it is that you need or want from Him. Oftentimes, we feel undeserving and unworthy to ask God for more. Romans 3:10 says, "As it is written, There is none righteous, no, not one." But God, being the awesome Father that He is, loves us so much that if we ask within His will, He will do it. Just like a parent provides for a child, God will give us what we need and want as long as it is what's best for us. Remember to go to God for everything; always keep the lines of communication open. Don't stop praying for any reason. Even if you can pray in your car on your way to work or in the shower, always take some time to acknowledge God.

Suggestion: During my fast, I found early morning as an awesome time to pray. Choose a quiet time where you can solely focus on God without distractions.

REFLECTIONS: Are you getting your daily prayer time in? Are you encouraging prayer with your family? What can you do to make personal and family prayer a priority in your life this week and going forward?

When is your designated prayer time?

What steps will you take to make prayer a priority for you and your family this week?

1. _____

2. _____

3. _____

WEEKLY CHALLENGE: Let all of your words and thoughts be positive for the entire week.

Day 2

Daily Prayer: *Lord, teach and guide me; show me how to fast and pray. I love You and thank You in advance, in Your name, Amen.* How do I fast-**Daily Scriptures**: Ezra 8:21-22 (NLT), Matthew 6:16-18

Discussion: In this particular passage, Ezra and the children of Israel were traveling back to Jerusalem from Babylon, and Ezra told the king that God protected everyone who worshipped Him. Ezra then realized this may be a dangerous journey but now he would have to literally walk out his faith. Ezra could not go back and ask the king for military protection from enemies along the way after proclaiming God's protection over His people. So he declared a fast; they humbled themselves and asked God to safeguard their passage into Jerusalem and God answered their prayers. It's of the utmost importance to know what you want from God, humble yourself and be specific when you ask. It is also important to know how to conduct yourself when fasting.

The sixth chapter of Matthew gives a clear explanation of the proper demeanor and behavior to display while fasting. Fasting is completely personal between you and God. The whole world should not know you are fasting; if you do let everyone know, that is your reward.

Day 3

: *Lord, thank You for your example of how to pray. I ask that You would teach me how to pray, in Jesus' name I pray, Amen.*

How do we pray-**Daily Scriptures**: Matthew 6:9-13, Psalm 109:1-31 (NKJV)

Discussion: In the book of Matthew, Jesus showed us how to pray with the Lord's Prayer. Jesus begins His prayer by exalting the name of the Lord and then acknowledging God's will as the only will to be done in heaven and earth. Jesus then asks for God to supply our daily needs, forgive our debts as we forgive others and deliver us from evil. Finally, He ends with more exaltation. This is a great example to follow when learning how to pray. There is also a good example of prayer written by David in Psalm 109. With David's prayer, the first 20 verses is David living out Luke 6:28, blessing and praying for his enemies: "Bless those who curse you, and pray for those who spitefully use you" (NKJV). We know that he was blessing them because of what he wrote in verses 4 and 5 of Psalm 109. He says, "In return for my love... they have rewarded me evil for good" (NKJV).

In general, when I consider Luke 6:28, I naturally think that praying for others means to wish well upon them. But in Psalm 109, David is praying for them to reap what they have sown. He is specific in what he would like to happen to them. The following 11 verses is David asking God for help. He says he was poor and needy and his heart was wounded, which are situations we all may have experienced at one time or another. He asks for help according to God's mercies and for Him to do it in such a way that everyone will know he was delivered by the hand of God. He then makes a point to praise God despite how he feels and while he's in the midst of his enemies.

Let us be mindful to pray for our enemies and go out of our way to bless them. Pray your way through and be the salt of the earth. The lives, attitudes and behavior of believers should be different. If the only difference between a Christian and a non-Christian is that Christians are in church on Sunday mornings, we are not salty enough. Dare to add some flavor to your life.

Day 4

Daily Prayer: *Dear Lord, help my unbelief. Help me to trust You in everything, in every area of my life, in Your name I pray, Amen.*

Trust and believe-**Daily Scriptures**: Proverbs 3:5, Matthew 21:22

Discussion: The foundation of Christianity itself is belief in Jesus Christ. If you do not believe John 3:16, then that is where you should start your journey. Without belief in God's Word, we will remain babes in Christ. Are you satisfied just making it in? Is it enough to accept Christ but not believe His Word? Life is filled with ups, downs, challenges, trials and tribulations. Being a Christian does not mean life will be easy; but if we believe what the Word of God says, it changes the prospective from which we view our situations and circumstances. When temptations come, we know that God will not allow us to be tempted with more than we can handle, and He will provide a way of escape so we can endure the temptation (1 Corinthians 10:13). When bad things happen and we may not understand why, believe that all things will work out for our good (Romans 8:28). Hold onto this truth and trust that God will see you through your situation.

Day 5

Daily Prayer: *Lord, I thank You and praise You for Your grace and mercy. Father, I pray for a clear understanding of Your Word that I may apply it to my life and be a blessing to others. Jesus, open my ears and my heart so I can hear directly from You, in Your name I pray, Amen.*

Examine your WHY for what you are asking-**Daily Scriptures**: James 4:3, Genesis 3:9

Discussion: What are the real reasons you are seeking God? Is what you are requesting in the will of God for your life? Do you envy the things or success of someone else? James clearly says that it is possible we have not received what we have asked of God because we are asking for selfish reasons. Examine your motivations for your fast and make sure that what you are asking for is within the will of God. In Genesis, God asked Adam, "Where art thou?" He was not asking Adam where he was because He did not know. He was asking to prompt Adam to make a self-evaluation and recognize what he was doing and where he was going. As you begin this journey, make a conscious effort to be honest with yourself during every aspect of this fast. Always reevaluate yourself and search for the most sincere and authentic responses.

What is your motivation for your request from God?

_____

_____

Who will benefit from God granting your request? How will they benefit?

_____

_____

Day 6

Daily Prayer: *Heavenly Father, my desire is to know You and recognize Your voice so I can follow You, in Jesus' name, Amen.*

Lord, is that You-**Daily Scriptures**: John 2:5, 10:27

Discussion: The second chapter of John describes the first miracle Jesus performed, turning water into wine. I heard a pastor say once that Mary sums up Christianity completely in that one verse: "Whatsoever he saith unto you, do it" (John 2:5). It seems so simple, but that is it in a nutshell. How do you recognize the voice of God? The same way you might recognize your mother's voice or your spouse or child: by spending time with them and talking to them everyday. The only way to get to know someone, God included, is to spend time with them. Learn the ways of God by learning the Word of God. Learn His voice by spending time in prayer. Be mindful not to always be the one talking. Don't confuse your voice for His.

Day 7

Daily Prayer: *Heavenly Father, show me the purpose You have planned for my life. Lord give me the strength and the courage to fulfill it, in Jesus' name, Amen.*

What is your purpose-**Daily Scriptures**: Ephesians 4:11-16 (NCV), Matthew 25:14-28, Habakkuk 2:2

Discussion: God has given us all a gift to be used for His glory. Have you identified your gift? If not, consider some things you enjoy doing or are really good at. Then see how you can apply those gifts and talents within the Body of Christ. Do you know what your gift is? Are you using it to build and edify the Body of Christ? Are you using it at all? Sometimes we can get caught up in our inadequacies, feeling like we are not good enough or cannot be of any use. Many times we over think things or allow fear to hinder us from exercising our gifts and talents. Have you ever heard that if you don't use it you'll lose it? Well, remember that in Matthew, the servant who buried the money in the ground instead of investing it to make more had that little that was given to him taken, and it was given to the one who doubled his money. I encourage you today to figure out what your gift, talent and purpose is. Once you know and understand your purpose, the next step is to write your vision and formulate a plan to bring your vision to pass. In the book of Habakkuk, the prophet was petitioning God to intervene into the situation of the people of Judah. God told Habakkuk exactly what was going to happen; He told him to write it down and make it plain so that the people would be able to apply it once they read it. Before an architect can begin construction, they must first have a blueprint. Prior to baking, a chef starts with a recipe just as we must write out our plans before we can execute them. Write out your purpose and your plan to fulfill it, then invest, exercise, develop and use it to the best of your ability unto the glory of God.

REFLECTIONS: What is your purpose? _____

_____

Are you actively pursuing your purpose?

_____

If not, what obstacles are you allowing to hinder you from walking in your purpose?

1._____

2._____

3._____

Do you think God was mistaken when He gave you your dreams and desires or that He can't use you? _____

God has a purpose for you; if you are unsure about what your purpose is, I encourage you to add your purpose to the list of fasting prayer requests. If you already know what your purpose is and are not working toward walking in it, list a solution for every obstacle you have written above.

1._____

2._____

3._____

Day 8

Daily Prayer: *Dear Lord, I thank You for your many blessings and I ask that You would strengthen and keep me so I can stay committed to You and this fast. Lord, let Your Word penetrate my heart and give me clear understanding. I thank You in advance for answering my prayers, and I ask all these things in the matchless name of Jesus, Amen.*

Stay committed even in the face of adversity-**Daily Scriptures:** Daniel 6

Discussion: Have you ever heard the saying, "If you dig one ditch, you better dig two cause the trap you set just might be for you"? Well, that is exactly what happened in the sixth chapter of Daniel. This story has many interesting and specific points to learn from. First, stay committed to God even when it's not popular or in this case, even when it's the law. Once Daniel was made aware of the decree that came down from King Darius, it was of no consequence to Daniel. He would not would abandon his faith and trust in God because of a law put in place to destroy him. Daniel had gotten to the place where he solely relied on God, so to suddenly begin living without acknowledging the presence of God was unfathomable.

Do you think of God that way? Do you see your relationship with Christ as the air you breathe? Another element to take note of is the level of Daniel's trust in God. Daniel was a high official; he knew the law and the consequences for breaking the law. When he became aware of the law, he did not try to hide. Daniel continued to openly worship God just as he had always done. Daniel had an unwavering resolve to honor and obey God despite the law of man. Once he was arrested, he didn't try to plead for his life or argue, he trusted. One of the most important points to recognize is the fact that God delivered Daniel. Daniel trusted and believed in God, and God delivered him from the lions den.

REFLECTIONS:

Do you have that type of faith and trust in God? List at least one example of this Daniel faith you have exercised some time during your spiritual walk.

_____

_____

_____

During this fast, fully commit and trust God so He can move on your behalf.

Day 9

Daily Prayer: *Lord, grant me the strength to fully commit to You and be obedient to You and Your Word. Open my ears, my mind and my heart so that I can hear You and recognize You when You speak. Lord, give me the faith to completely trust You, in Jesus' name I pray, Amen.*

Make sure there's gas in your tank-**Daily Scriptures**: James 2:14-26

Discussion: Having a brand new car with new tires, new rims and tinted windows is a blessing; but until there is gas in the car, it will not move. The same analogy can be applied to faith. Even with all the faith in the world, without action, there is just faith: no motion, no advancement and no progress. People often say, I am waiting on the Lord, but there are things you can do while you wait for God to move. For example, believing God to bless your career so you can become a world renowned race car driver but not learning how to drive is a prime illustration of James 2:26 which says that faith without works is dead. This may seem extreme, but the point is that progress requires action. There is a common phrase within the Christian community, "Step out on faith." The word step is an action word, indicating movement in a particular direction toward specific goals or desires. Fasting is a step of faith; it demonstrates trust in the Word of God and the belief that God is willing and able to move on your behalf. Are you asking for God to do something in your life but you have not done your part? When we step or move towards God's purpose for our lives, we are exercising our faith: putting gas in the car. We enable God to move on our behalf; when we move, He moves just like that!

REFLECTIONS: Are you believing God for something?

_____

Are you waiting for God to move or are you actively waiting?

_____

What steps can you take to move toward your purpose?

1._____

2._____

3._____

WEEKLY CHALLENGE: Remove one distraction from your routine this week. For example, TV, video games, social media or anything that takes away from spiritual or developmental growth.

Day 10

Daily Prayer: *Father God, I thank You for another day and ask that You give me the courage to trust You and follow You even if I'm afraid. All this I ask in Jesus' name, Amen.*

Have faith, trust God and move forward even if you are afraid-**Daily Scriptures**: Judges 6 & 7

Discussion: This story about Gideon is quite interesting as it reflects a common journey that a Christian experiences during spiritual growth. Becoming a Christian only takes a belief (Romans 10:9); spiritual growth and maturity is a quest that occurs over time as a result of faith and trust in God while maneuvering through life. Everyone within the Body of Christ at some point has felt unsure about the course that God was directing them to and felt a need to ask God for confirmation. The Creator knows His creations; God thoroughly knows and understands each individual personally. He is aware of every insecurity and can position and prepare every single member of the Body of Christ willing to be used by Him for His glory.

For example, Gideon received specific instruction from God but still felt unsure. Gideon's uncertainty prompted him to ask God for a definitive sign confirming that his conversation was indeed with God. God desires to have a trustworthy relationship with His children. Christians serve as the actual Body of Christ. Operating as His hands and feet, God has to be able to trust His Body to obey and live His Word with the spirit of love. God recognizes human inadequacy, including doubt, and He understands the journey necessary to build trust. Therefore, He will accommodate any request that will strengthen the faith and build the trust of His children as He did with Gideon.

REFLECTIONS:

Have you ever been in a situation where God told you to do something and you were unsure of what He said? Did you ask for confirmation?

_____

_____

It is totally acceptable to ask God for confirmation or clarity. Remember, God is our loving Father and wants us come to Him with our concerns and problems. If we have a willing heart, God will work with us on our terms to accomplish His will. I want to encourage you to have faith and even if you are afraid, still trust God, be obedient and do what God wants you to do.

Day 11

Daily Prayer: *Lord, show me how trust and depend on You in every situation I may face. I thank You in advance, in Jesus' name, Amen.*

Surviving life's situations-**Daily Scriptures**: Luke 22:39-44(NLT), Jeremiah 29:11-13, 1 Corinthians 10:13

Discussion: The 22nd chapter of Luke explains how to deal with life's difficulties. In verse 39, Jesus takes the disciples to the mount of Olives to pray. Luke intentionally says, "and went as usual" (NLT). This establishes the importance of an active prayer life. When your prayer life is lacking or non existent, it is the equivalent of walking around alone in the dark. You have no direction and no guidance, and you're stagnant and unmoving. We all have a purpose; God has a plan for us all and He already has our expected end. All we have to do is accept, believe and obey Him: a simple recipe for our success. Next, Jesus warned His disciples to pray that they don't enter into temptation. Temptation will come but know this:

1. You are not the only person to go through this.
2. We will not be temped above what we are able.
3. God will make a way of escape so we can bear it.

Further within this scripture, notice how Christ's vulnerability as a man is revealed as He asks God the Father if He is willing to remove this cup from Him. His flesh does not want to face His impending crucifixion. There are times when we have to go through difficult times. Christ prayed through this difficult time and asked for God's will, not His to be done. How many times have you allowed difficult circumstances to move you out of the will of God?

29

Sometimes when you pray, you need to be prepared for God to tell you something you did not want to hear. But know and understand that God wants what's best for you more than you want what's best for you; and whatever you go through is ultimately going to benefit you and move you to another level. Don't allow situations, circumstances, trials, tribulations, difficulties or people to discourage, hinder or deter you from your divine purpose.

Day 12

Daily Prayer: *Lord show me my sin, if there is anything within me that is not like you, reveal it and give me the strength to remove it from my life, in Jesus' name, Amen.*

What sin is blocking your full potential for your life-**Daily Scriptures**: Psalm 66:18 (NLT), Psalm 32:3-5, Proverbs 28:13, James 4:3 (KJV), James 1:5-8, Romans 14:23, Isaiah 59:1-2 (NLT), Romans 1:28 (CEV), Luke 6:38, Matthew 6:12, Mark 11:25 (NLT), Matthew 6:14-15 (NLT), Colossians 3:13 (NLT), Luke 6:37

Discussion: Is sin hindering your prayers from being answered? What sin is preventing you from receiving all that God has for you? Is it unforgiveness, lust, self-indulgence, over-indulgence, disobedience, pride or selfishness? On a daily basis, Christians should establish a measure of self-assessment while petitioning God for revelation of sin to identify what is obstructing the growth, prayers and blessings of the Body of Christ. In Isaiah, it states that the problem is not that God cannot hear you or He is unable or unwilling, it's because we have allowed our sin to build a wall between us and God and move us farther away from Him. Think of sin as a brick and every time we sin, a brick is being laid one on top of another. Initially with the first few bricks, the Holy Spirit will get our attention to bring awareness to what we are doing so we can repent and turn away from that particular sin. But as we continue to sin, we continue to build the wall; and before long, we have been completely separated from God and He has given us over to a reprobate mind. Sin will hinder your progress.

Being stingy will hinder your blessings. God has established a principle that if you give, more will be given back to you. If you have an opportunity to research some of the richest people in the world, one thing you will find is that they are very generous and understand that the more they give, the more that comes back to them. How can you receive with a closed fist?

31

Doubt will block your blessings. James says that a double-minded man is unstable and if you doubt, do not expect to receive anything from God. Faith is the key that can unlock so much in the spiritual realm; don't allow your blessings to be trapped by the door of doubt after you have already unlocked it.

Unforgiveness will block your blessings. When Jesus was teaching us the Lord's prayer, He made a point to say forgive us our debts AS WE forgive our debtors. Forgiveness is necessary for God to forgive us. Also, forgiveness is for us. When we forgive, we allow healing to occur. Release any unforgiveness so you can move forward with what God has for you. Let's not allow sin, stinginess, doubt or unforgiveness to keep us from moving higher in Christ and becoming everything He has for us to become.

Psalm 66:18 (NLT) clearly says, "If I had not confessed the sin in my heart, the Lord would not have listened." When God reveals your hidden and not-so-hidden sin, take the following steps in 2 Chronicles 7:14 to address sin:

1. Acknowledge it
2. Address it
3. Turn from it

James explains that many times we have not received an answer from God because we asked based upon our lust. Do not continue to allow sin to intercept the abundance and fullness God has for your life.

Suggestion: Make a conscious effort to apply these steps: examine, recognize, confess and repent as a part of your daily routine to experience the fullness of God.

REFLECTIONS: Have you experienced a time when you were convicted about sin? _____

Were you receptive or did you immediately deny it? _____

Did you become angry with God or with the person God sent to talk to you about your sin? Why or why not? _____

_____

Day 13

Daily Prayer: *Father, I trust you to mold and shape me into what You would have me to be. I understand that it may not feel good, but I submit my will to Yours and pray that You will use me in spite of my flaws and short comings, in Jesus' name, Amen.*

God hears, listens and responds when we obey-**Daily Scriptures**: Joshua 10:1-14 (NIV)

Discussion: Obedience creates a perfect environment for God to hear and answer our prayers. Consider a parent/child relationship; if you had a child who did everything you asked, it would be easy for you to grant a request from them as long as it was beneficial and not detrimental. In this story, the Lord told Joshua that He would deliver the Amorites into his hand. Joshua asked the Lord to stop the sun and the moon so that they could finish defeating their enemies. Joshua was doing what God required so why would God deny his request? Disobedience ties the hands of God. In 1 Samuel 15:22 (NIV), Samuel says, "to obey is better than sacrifice." Make sure this fast is not a sacrifice while you are still being disobedient to the voice of God. Examine yourself and be sure the obstacle blocking your blessings is not your disobedience.

REFLECTIONS: Has God given you a specific task? Are you doing it or are you running from it?

_____

_____

Day 14

: *Lord, I pray that you would allow me to draw closer to You. Lord, give me clarity and wisdom as I strive to know You more through Your Word. Lord, I long to have a deeper understanding of You and a more intimate relationship, in Jesus' name, Amen.*

Venture into the deep -**Daily Scriptures**: James 4:8, Hebrews 5:12-14, 11:6, Luke 5:4, Colossians 3:16

Discussion: Salvation is the only thing in this life in which we can get something for nothing. Acquiring salvation is simple: Romans 10:9 says that if you confess with your mouth the Lord Jesus and believe in your heart that God raised Him from the dead, you will be saved. At that moment, you are saved and are a babe in Christ with no knowledge or understanding of the Word or the things of God. Is it enough to just make it in and remain a babe in Christ?

If you were to examine the type of Christian you are, would you be a superficial Christian who can quote scripture but have no application of it? A surface Christian who can only be recognized as a Christian on Sunday mornings? An immature Christian who has asked Christ to come into your heart but not to be Lord of your life? It is perfectly normal to be in one of these categories at some point as a developing Christian. What is important is to continue progressing and growing. If you are reading this book, then you are on the right track to cultivating a deeper relationship with Christ. James 4:8 says, "Draw nigh to God, and he will draw nigh to you." Recognize that the ball is your court; the game begins when you begin to move closer to Christ.

Just as children grow up, we too as Christians should grow and mature spiritually. Children have to be told instructions over and over again; they cannot be left on their own or accept responsibility for anyone or anything else.

Mature Christians should be able to lead others to Christ and share and explain the Word of God. Someone's life could be dependent upon your testimony and commitment to Christ. Hebrews 11:6 says that God rewards those who diligently seek Him; think of the things you are diligent about. Is Christ one of them? It may be necessary to reprioritize some things in your life if you are not diligently seeking after Christ and the things of God. Luke shares Peter's fishing experience where Christ instructed him to go into the deep and let down his nets. To receive the great multitude of fish, it is necessary to go deeper. You may be able to survive on what you catch from the surface; but to be full and nourished, you must delve into deeper waters. Get your nets and launch out into the deep.

: *Holy Spirit, I pray that you would guide me throughout my day and give me the strength and presence of mind to trust You even when I can't hear You, in Jesus' name I pray, Amen.*

When God is silent, He may want to see how badly you want it-
Daily Scriptures: Matthew 15:21-28, Mark 7:24-30

Discussion: Life sometimes has a way of challenging you to the point where you may have to fight for what you want. Not in the traditional sense of the word that suggests anger and violence, but meaning to not give up, not surrender until you have received what you need. From this story told by both Matthew and Mark we see multiple lessons that can be applied to everyday life. This particular woman came to Christ because she needed something specific and she knew He was the only one who could help her. When she first encountered Christ, He ignored her (Matthew 15:23). Despite that, she didn't stop; she was fighting for the life of her daughter. At this point, she was begging for Christ to help her and His response, because she was a Gentile, was that He was sent to help the people of Israel. She had an expectation and would not stop until she received at the very least a reason why He would not help her. Do not allow people to keep you from your destiny because of what they think of your pedigree or who they think you are or believe you to be. Maybe you weren't born into a wealthy family or didn't have the best education, but God has a purpose and a plan for your life. Do not be discouraged the first or the tenth time you hear the word "no." God may be strengthening your character and resilience for things to come. You may need to draw from this experience to get through to the next one on your journey to reaching your destiny. If God sees you give up after the first road block you come to, then He knows you won't be ready to handle more difficult things you may encounter in the future. Don't be afraid to fight for what you know God has destined for you to do. Never give up on the dream God has given you. Following your purpose will likely inspire or impact someone else's life in a way you had not considered, but God did. Put your gloves on and get ready for round one.

Day 16

Daily Prayer: *Heavenly Father, I ask that You give me the ability to recognize when I need to change and adjust appropriately in every situation.*

Adjust your attitude-**Daily Scriptures**: Matthew 15:21-28, Mark 7:24-30

Discussion: Certain situations may require a particular attitude to produce a desired outcome. This discussion is a continuation of yesterday's scripture about the Syrophoenician woman who sought Jesus to deliver her daughter from demonic possession. After being ignored and then told that Jesus was sent for the children of Israel, a group she did not belong to, she realized that she needed to change her approach. She recognized Christ for who He was and adjusted from a posture of pleading to a posture of worship. Her decision to submit her pride and worship put her in a position to receive what she needed from Christ. Most of us when faced with a situation where we feel disrespected would quickly become annoyed, frustrated and maybe even angry. This woman demonstrated self-control and humility because what was at stake was bigger than her pride. Pray for the wisdom to act appropriately in every situation, always knowing when and how respond.

Day 17

Daily Prayer: *Lord, I ask You to help me to bridle my tongue and always speak with a spirit of love. Help me to be slow to anger and think before I speak, in Jesus' name, Amen.*

Watch your mouth-**Daily Scriptures**: James 3:3-12 (NIV), James 1:19, 26 (NLT), Proverbs 15:1, 18:21, Psalm 34:13 (NLT)

Discussion: As Christians, it is imperative to always be mindful about the words that we allow to leave our lips. Once something has been said, you can't take it back. As a part of the Body of Christ, we never want to hurt someone with our words or even with the tone of our voice. James explains how powerful the tongue is and why we have to keep a tight reign on it. Proverbs 18:21 says that life and death is in the power of the tongue; take every opportunity to speak life, not death, and to encourage, not discourage. It's better to hold your tongue than to say something that creates hurt, distrust, anger and eventually apologize later. Please let the words that come from your mouth be saturated with love and kindness.

WEEKLY CHALLENGE: Do some form of physical activity everyday this week for a minimum of 15 minutes. It does not have to be strenuous; take a walk, ride a bike or turn the radio to your favorite station and just dance. Let's get moving.

Day 18

Daily Prayer: *Thank You, Lord, for another opportunity to be better than I was yesterday. Lord, help me to hear and understand Your Word. Fix my heart, Lord, so I may be a blessing to someone else. Remove anything not like You and help me to always give Your name praise, in Jesus' name, Amen.*

Keep talking no matter what-**Daily Scriptures:** Jonah 4

Discussion: This chapter of Jonah is particularly noteworthy in that it demonstrates active communication during a time when Jonah was upset with God. There may be times in life that seem unfair. Circumstances may occur that might cause you to feel hurt or lost, and it is a perfectly normal reaction to get upset with God. During these times, although you feel anger or frustration towards God, just continue talking to Him, continue praying. When Jonah disobeyed God's direct orders, he still prayed and told God why he was disobedient and upset with God. Then God took the time to show Jonah why He is God and explain why He chose to do what He did. God doesn't have to explain anything but if you ask, He will, just like He did with Jonah. God wants a relationship with us and to develop a relationship, there must be communication. Communication is the key to every successful relationship - a friendship, familial relationship, romantic relationship or your relationship with Christ - that fact does not change. No matter what, just keep talking.

REFLECTIONS: How do you respond to sudden, unplanned or hurtful events? _____

Do you allow the event to effect the way you relate to God? _____

_____

Can you recall a time when you were upset with God? Did you withdraw from the presence of God or draw closer to Him? _____

_____

Day 19

Daily Prayer: *Dear Lord, help me to stay focused on what You have for me to do. Jesus, help me to recognize distractions so I can remove them from my life and move forward with Your plan for me. I thank You in advance and pray all these things in Your name, Amen.*

Stay focused and run your race-**Daily Scriptures**: Hebrews 12:1-12 (NLT), Proverbs 16:3 (NLT), James 1:2-4

Discussion: Sometimes we have days when we can be totally focused and productive; then there are other times when we allow things, situations and circumstances to distract us. Hebrews reminds us to lay aside every weight, every sin and anything that may be hindering our progress towards completing our God-given purpose. We also learn here that everything happens for a reason; and just like our children need correction, we as children of God need correcting as well from time to time. Understand that correction is for our good. James tells us to count it all joy because the testing of our faith produces patience. God always has a plan to get us to an expected end. To be able to stay focused and follow Christ when we cannot see the path or the relevance of what is happening requires daily prayer and worship. When you have an active prayer life, the Holy Spirit will guide you and show you, so you are not walking blind. God will reveal to you when things are distractions and urge you to refocus. Having an active prayer life is like a child bowling with the bumpers in the gutter lane: when the ball (us) veers off course towards the gutter, the bumpers (Holy Spirit) steer the ball (us) back in the right direction.

Day 20

Daily Prayer: *Heavenly Father, I pray that You would grant me the wisdom to make wise decisions, seek wise counsel, use discernment and have the courage to listen and follow Your guidance, in the mighty name of Jesus, Amen.*

If you need wisdom, ask **-Daily Scriptures**: Matthew 25:1-13 (NCV), Proverbs 6: 6-8, Psalm 1:1-3 (NLT), James 1:1-8

Discussion: In everything we do, we must use wisdom. God gave us all a measure of common sense. Always make measured decisions; in other words, be thoughtful about what you do. Like the parable of the virgins in Matthew, the wise virgins brought extra oil just in case. They had the foresight to plan ahead. When you have the time and opportunity to plan ahead, it just makes sense to do so. If you need help, seek wise counsel, not the counsel referred to in Psalm 1. James 1:5 says that if we need wisdom, all we have to do is ask. Jesus gave us the Holy Spirit to guide us. We are not in this alone; we have help so use it.

Day 21

Daily Prayer: *Heavenly Father, help me to recognize anything that may be hindering me from doing Your will. Lord, give me the strength to remove all distractions so I can learn, grow and be productive for the Body of Christ, in Jesus' name, Amen.*

Lay aside every weight-**Daily Scriptures**: Hebrews 12:1 (NLT)

Discussion: What are you carrying around that may be hindering your growth or progress? Paul makes a point to tell us to lay aside every weight and the sin that so easily entraps us. With the advancement of smart phones, technology has permitted access to instantaneous information literally at our fingertips. This progress has also created easy accessibility to many distractions by way of social media, apps, games, texts, emails or maybe just watching too much TV. Think about the time you spend on Facebook or Instagram: What else could you being with that time? What is God's calling on your life? People make time for what is established as a priority. The statement, "I don't have time" really means I am not willing to make that particular thing a priority. Considering Christians are the Body of Christ and operate has His hands and feet, spiritual preparation is essential in the event God calls upon His Body to be a witness for Him, encourage someone or just show love to someone who is hurting. Without studying, it is impossible to possess the knowledge of God's Word to pour into anyone else. Without prayer, our hearts may not be ready to help comfort someone else when we may feel bad ourselves. Prayer is the pathway to communicate with God. An active prayer life allows direct communication with God, which enables the ability to receive clear direction and instruction. Study and prayer is critical for every disciple of Christ. Be mindful of the weights you carry. There's nothing worse than missing an opportunity because you were not prepared.

REFLECTIONS: How much time in hours per day do you spend on social media? _____

How many hours per day do you spend watching TV?

_____

How much time is that combined per week? _____ per month?
_____ per year? _____

Make of list of what you could have spent your time doing.

_____

_____

_____

_____

_____

Make a list of things you could have accomplished had you spent
your time doing what you wrote on the previous list.

_____

_____

_____

_____

_____

ACTION: Write at least one adjustment you will make to your daily
routine to move toward accomplishing one item from the previous
list.

_____

Day 22

Daily Prayer: *Lord, I pray that You would help me be a better communicator so I can have a deeper relationship with You, in Jesus' name I pray, Amen.*

The power of the Holy Spirit-**Daily Scriptures**: Romans 8 (NLT)

Discussion: Recently, I was asked why God had to send His Son to die for us and the answer was in Romans 8:3. A sacrifice had to be made and Jesus was the only one pure, holy and willing to give His life to save ours. For those who may be struggling with a particular sin for a seemingly long time, this chapter can assist with that. The key is to surrender your will and allow the Holy Spirit to take control; verse 6 says that will lead us to life and peace. Christ granted us release from the control of sin through His death and resurrection. This only occurs when we submit our lives fully and allow the Spirit to lead us. God has accepted Christians as joint heirs with Christ with direct access to the Father through the Son. We are no longer slaves to the appetite of the flesh - lust, anger, judgments, addictions or anything else that we allow to rule within us. Verse 26 says that the Holy Spirit helps us in our weakness by praying for us with groanings that cannot be expressed in words. When you pray, you don't always have to speak; sometimes you need to be still and listen. How can you hear what the Lord is saying if you're always talking? Sometimes we may have to groan and permit the Holy Spirit to intercede for us and speak directly to God because He knows what we need better than we do. The last eight verses of the chapter talk about the awesome love of God and how we cannot be separated from it. How many times have you heard about family members who don't speak because of something that happened 10 years ago and they probably don't even remember what it was? Using the example of how God loves us, this should never happen within our own families or within the Body of Christ.

REFLECTIONS: Is there an area of life that you have not totally entrusted to Christ? For example, your health: Are you taking care of His temple? Your business: Have you trusted your business to God? Your marriage: Is God the head of your union? List anything that you have not yet given fully to Christ.

1._____

2._____

3._____

What is hindering you from letting go and trusting God in those areas?

1._____

2._____

3._____

Day 23

<u>Daily prayer</u>: *Lord, give me the strength to be slow to anger, slow to speak and trust You to handle any situation that may arise. Jesus, help me to show Your love for Your people, so others will see You in everything that I do, in Your name, Amen.*

Love in spite of-**Daily Scriptures**: Romans 12:2, Mark 12:31, Proverbs 15:1-5

<u>Discussion</u>: As Christians, our lives should reflect the love of Jesus in our speech, attitudes, actions and perspectives. Oftentimes we are challenged and tested by co-workers, our children, spouses and friends. During those times, we must be able to withhold our fleshly reaction and draw on the power of God to be able to respond with a spirit of love. Proverbs tells us that a kind word or response turns away wrath. Trying times will reveal the spiritual maturity level of a Christian. Your reaction and response to difficult situations and trials can be an indication of the time spent in prayer and studying the Word of God. Are you able to love in spite of how you're being treated or spoken to? This by no means says that Christians must be silent and endure mistreatment and disrespect. It means that we control our reactions and when we do respond, it is in a wise and Spirit-led manner. Practice loving in spite of every opportunity you have to retaliate.

REFLECTIONS: Can you recall a time whn you had to love someone who did not treat you well? Did you love them in spite of how you were treated? What did you do to show love despite how you felt?

_____

_____

_____

Day 24

Daily Prayer: *Dear Lord, help me to have the courage and boldness to share Your goodness with everyone I come in contact with. Let me be an example of You as I go about my daily routine in life. Help me to always reflect You even when I am experiencing difficult times, in Jesus' name I pray, Amen.*

Be bold and share Christ; lives are at stake-**Daily Scriptures**: Mark 16:15-16, Matthew 28:19-20, 1 Timothy 4:12, 2 Corinthians 3:2-3 (NASB)

Discussion: In Matthew 4:19, Jesus says, "Follow me, and I will make you fishers of men." To become a fisher of men, it is important to use love as bait and be an example. It can be as simple as not using profanity in your everyday speech; responding with a genuine "Thank You Lord" or "Praise the Lord" when recognizing a blessing; being positive and uplifting and eliminating negativity from your conversation; or being sanctified which in essence, means to be set apart. There should be something that differentiates you from everyone else because of your Christianity. When you exhibit the characteristics of Christ, people will take notice and may wonder, inquire or reason why you're "so nice." Second Corinthians 3:2-3 clearly says that we are the living example of God's Word. We may be the only Bible some people ever read.

WEEKLY CHALLENGE: Step out of your comfort zone and do something out of the ordinary. Go sing karaoke, introduce yourself to someone you don't know or share your thoughts and feelings during Sunday school or bible study. Stretch yourself a bit; you might like it.

Day 25

Daily Prayer: *Dear Lord, allow me to see with Your eyes, think with the mind of Christ and feel with Your heart. Heavenly Father, I pray that You would give me the means, talent, vision and ability to be Your hands and feet and be a blessing to Your people, in Jesus' name, Amen.*

"If we are the Body, why aren't His arms reaching?" Casting Crowns-**Daily Scriptures**: Romans 12:5, 1 Corinthians 12:12-31 (NIV), Mark 12:31, 2 Corinthians 3:3 (NLT)

Discussion: I love this song by Casting Crowns; it simply says that if we are the Body of Christ, why aren't His arms reaching, His hands healing, His words teaching, His feet going, His love not showing them there is a way. We are literally the Body of Christ. We have been given the task of loving our neighbors as we love ourselves. This includes everyone, not just people who look like us, work with us or are related to us. There are so many opportunities to share Christ with someone by your actions. We have to be promoters of Christ and spread His love wherever we can. This may be a simple act of kindness, a smile, a kind word or a hug. Sometimes just lending an ear or sitting with someone may be comforting to them. You don't have to be rich or a bible scholar to be a blessing to someone. If everyone looked out for someone else, we would all be taken care of.

Day 26

Daily Prayer: *Dear Lord, show me how to love everyone like You do, in Jesus' name, Amen.*

Are you a Good Samaritan-**Daily Scriptures**: Luke 10:25-37 (NLT)

Discussion: This story contains many points of interest. The law expert essentially asked Jesus for a checklist to point out the specific tasks necessary to qualify as loving your neighbor, as if to say that loving your neighbor can be confined to a certain number of tasks. Love cannot be encompassed by guidelines, borders or limitations. Love is limitless; love goes above and beyond a normal or reasonable expectation, which Jesus demonstrates in His parable about the Good Samaritan.

This particular road from Jerusalem to Jericho was obviously quite dangerous since the story begins with a Jewish man who was robbed, beaten and left for dead on the side of the road. Jesus goes on to say that not only one but two men, both of whom were supposed to be representatives of God (a priest and a Levite), crossed to the other side of the road when they saw this man lying in the street. It is possible these men realized how dangerous this road was and wanted to avoid the same fate. It is also possible that they were in a hurry to reach their destination. Maybe they felt they were not in a position to help him. Whatever the reason, their behavior was not an example of how to love your neighbor. Would you have stopped to show compassion to this person in need? Well, a Good Samaritan did. At this time in history, the Jews abhorred the Samaritans so Jesus described him as a despised Samaritan. He not only stopped to see about him, he cared for his wounds, put the man on his donkey, took him to an inn and cared for him there. Then the following day, he instructed and paid the inn keeper to look after him until his return. The story ends with Jesus asking the lawyer that of the three men in the story who saw the man attacked by bandits, who acted as a good neighbor? The lawyer's response was, "The one who showed him mercy." Are you the one who shows mercy?

Day 27

Daily prayer: *Heavenly Father, I pray that You would help me be grateful for everything that happens in my life. Lord, remind me to be thankful and not complain, but count everything joy. And help me to recognize that everything has a purpose, and trials come to make me better and stronger for You. I love You, in the mighty name of Jesus Christ, Amen.*

Be grateful and count it all joy-**Daily Scriptures**: 1 Thessalonians 5:18, Psalm 118:1, James 2:2-4, James 1: 2-3 (CEV), Romans 8:28, Genesis 37, 39, 40, 41:1-44

Discussion: We often have days when it seems like whatever can go wrong, does go wrong. When we have days like that, we can sometimes focus on the situation or how the circumstance is making us feel. I encourage you not to focus on those things but recognize the blessings hidden within your circumstance. Keep in mind that you may not understand how things will work out for your good at this particular moment, but they will somehow work out to benefit you. Joseph is a prime example of Romans 8:28. After being betrayed by his brothers, sold into slavery, lied on and imprisoned, Joseph eventually became the second most powerful man in Egypt behind Pharaoh. God favored Joseph throughout his entire journey. At each step, God blessed everything Joseph did. He was always placed in a position of authority that was training for what was to come. The next time you find yourself in a difficult situation, remember Joseph, count it all joy and it will work out for your good in due time. You may not be able to see how right now, but trust and believe God that it will work out. That is one of the perks to being a King's kid. Are you a complainer? Do you see the glass as half empty or half full?

SUGGESTIONS: The next time you begin to complain, stop immediately and tell God "thank you." Allow your joy for the Lord to be your strength.

Day 28

Daily Prayer: *Dear Lord, help me to understand Your Word and have the faith to trust You and believe Your Word, in Jesus' name, Amen.*

Should you pay your tithes? Absolutely NOT-**Daily Scriptures**: Malachi 3:6-10, 2 Corinthians 9:6-12 (NLT), Proverbs 3:9-10, Leviticus 27:30.

Discussion: Should you pay your tithes? No, you should not pay your tithes, you should cheerfully give your tithes. Tithing is a faithful act of obedience. Proverbs 3:9 says we should honor God with our first fruits and Leviticus tells us that our tithe is holy. When we tithe, we are saying that no matter what is going on in our lives, we trust God to provide and supply all of our needs. Because tithing is a faith act, God assures us that if we are obedient tithers, He will bless us as He encourages us to "prove me now herewith, saith the Lord of hosts, if I will not open you the windows of heaven, and pour you out a blessing, that there shall not be room enough to receive it"(Malachi 3:10). Tithing allows us to exercise our faith, building trust and strengthening our relationship with God. Tithing is an awesome expression of faith and obedience. Many people struggle with tithing for various reasons. I have listed some of the reservations I had in the past and how I overcame them:

1. What were they going to do with my money? Malachi helped me understand that I was giving my offering unto God and not man; it was not my concern what happened to the funds after I gave them to God. The ones responsible for the money would be accountable to God for how they managed it, but my commitment was to obey God and cheerfully give my tithe.
2. Should I tithe from my gross or my net? Well, I realized that God provided me with my entire paycheck, not just what I had left over after taxes. God should get the first fruit. I began to tithe off my gross, not my net, immediately after I got paid. I also recognized that it was necessary for me to remove and give it immediately because life happens and something could arise that would tempt me to use it for another purpose. The tithe is your seed; once you give or plant your seed, God can bless it to

grow and produce fruit. I did not want to waste my seed and have nothing to harvest later.

3. Will I have enough money to do everything that I need to with my check? I have learned that when you trust God and believe His Word, He is faithful to do what He said He would do. There have been times when I didn't know how things would work out but during those times, I would pray and recite God's Word back to Him. For example, I might say, "Lord, You said in Philippians 4:19 that You would supply all my needs according to Your riches in glory by Christ Jesus. Lord, You said that all things work together for good to them love You and are called according to Your purpose (Romans 8:28)." Then I would let God know that I was trusting Him; I would close my prayer with thanks for what God was getting ready to do. My outcome was that God did just what He said. He has continually blessed me and met every one of my needs, and I believe it's due to trusting in God to be faithful to His Word. Remember, Numbers 23:19 says, God is not a man that He should lie; God comes through every time, no matter what.

REFLECTIONS: Do you have any doubts or hesitation concerning tithing? If so, list what concerns you have regarding tithing.

1.

_____

2.

_____

3.

_____

4.

_____

Now research in what the Word of God says regarding your concerns.

1._____

_____

2. _____

_____

3. _____

_____

4. _____

_____

Day 29

Daily Prayer: *Lord, help me to exercise self-control in every area of my life. I thank You for the fruit of the Spirit and the strength to resist and overcome my fleshly desires, in Jesus' name, Amen.*

Self-control-**Daily Scriptures**: 1 Thessalonians 4:4 (NCV), Galatians 5:19-23 (NLT), Romans 8:9 (NLT), Proverbs 25:28

Discussion: Self-control can be a difficult task when not led by the Holy Spirit. Proverbs says that someone without self-discipline is like a city without walls. What are the risks of having an unprotected city? A city without walls is left open and vulnerable to attacks without any outside protection. If Christians lacked self-control, God's community would operate in a "no holds barred" environment where everything goes, nothing is off limits and no boundaries exist. This sounds somewhat extreme but consider if there was just one area of your life that you conducted in a constant state of permissiveness. What would be the ramifications? Would you be an alcoholic, have a nasty attitude or perhaps, be overweight? First Thessalonians says that God wants us to learn how to manage and control our own bodies. Learning self-control is a process that occurs over time by actively exercising self-control. In general, learning requires time devoted to studying a particular subject. God has given us His Word to study, learn and use as a guide. In Galatians, Paul writes that God has given us self-control as part of the fruit of the Spirit. That means as Christians, we all have the ability to display self-control. Just like a body builder exercises to strengthen his muscles, the Body of Christ must exercise self-control over the tongue, lusts and the flesh. Be deliberate in studying God's Word and spending time in prayer to be fully equipped to demonstrate self-control.

REFLECTIONS: List some areas of your life that may be lacking self-control.

1. _____

2. _____

3. _____

What action will you take to improve in those areas?

1. _____

2. _____

3. _____

Day 30

Daily Prayer: *Heavenly Father, I pray that You would give me the courage and tenacity to stand up for Your Word and Your will. Help me to always do what is right in Your sight. Also, Lord, I pray that You would give me the strength and power to withstand any trials that may come as a result of standing on Your Word, in Jesus' name, Amen.*

Stand up for Christ-**Daily Scriptures**: Numbers 25 (NLT), Romans 1:16, Luke 9:26, Colossians 2:8, Matthew 15:3-9, 1 Peter 2:9, Mark 8:38, Mark 14:29-31, 66-72, Ephesians 6:10-13

Discussion: As Christians, First Peter tells us that we are a peculiar people, a chosen generation. There should be a clear distinction between us and someone who does not have a personal relationship with Christ. Our Christianity should be recognizable by our speech, behavior and character. Being a Christian means sometimes having to go against the social norms or accepting society's popular trends because they do not agree with the Word of God. Ephesians tells us to be strong in the Lord and prepare by putting on the full armor of God, because there will come a time when we will have to stand against the wiles of the devil. The story in Numbers speaks about one man who stood up for God when His law was being blatantly disrespected. As a result, God rewarded this young man, whose name is Phinehas, with a special covenant that gave him and his descendants a permanent right to priesthood.

Have you ever been in a situation where you had to take a stand against what was popular or a societal norm? As Christians, there will come a time when we will have to stand on the Word of God, opposite of what the majority says is right. Just watching TV may require a spiritual decision with our modern society's casual acceptance of profanity, sexual innuendos and homosexuality.

Many times because of the acceptance of tradition, Christians may compromise the Gospel without even recognizing it. It is acceptable to tell children about Santa Claus, the Easter Bunny and the Tooth Fairy. Are those "stories" and not lies, some of which defer the actual meaning about Christ to a non-Christian figure? Is participating in Halloween a concession of the Gospel? These are just some questions to provoke you to reconsider some common practices that we have deemed acceptable that might be a compromise of the Word of God. Given the opportunity, would you stand up with a spirit of Phinehas or cower like Peter? Christ is clear: if we are ashamed of Him, He will be ashamed of us when He returns. Make sure you are standing on the right side; chose wisely.

WEEKLY CHALLENGE: Do something for someone else every day this week. Cook dinner for a friend, leave a nice note on your co-workers desk, smile, give someone a hug, be a good listener or go out of your way a little to bless someone else.

Day 31

Daily Prayer: *Dear Lord, I pray that You would help me to recognize what season I'm in. Lord, I ask You to guide and direct my path so I can please You in everything that I do, in Jesus' name, Amen.*

What season are you in-**Daily Scriptures**: Ecclesiastes 3:1-8

Discussion: What season are you in? Understanding what stage your life is in can be essential for your success. Like a farmer needs to know when to plant and when to harvest, we too need to know what season our lives are in. You may be in a preparatory stage where you are studying or perfecting a skill, gift or talent God has called you to. Winter season could be the time when you are focusing and pressing to reach your goal, and it may seem extremely difficult and quite possibly lonely. Be comforted knowing that when the frost subsides, you will be ready to blossom into your calling. The important thing is to recognize which season you're in. You do not want to enter into your spring season totally unprepared because you were unaware it was time for winter preparation.

Day 32

Daily Prayer: *Dear Lord, give me the heart to forgive those who have hurt me and the courage to ask for forgiveness of those I may have hurt, in Jesus' name I pray, Amen.*

Unforgiveness-**Daily Scriptures**: Matthew 6:14-15, 1 John 1:9

Discussion: Many of us have scars from past hurts or wounds caused by other people. We may have at one time or another become a recipient of anger, abuse or neglect that affected us so deeply that we may have developed bitterness, wrath, resentment and possibly hatred toward the person who offended us. I am sure you have heard the saying, forgive and forget, but that statement is much easier said than done. Unforgiveness can eat away at us from the inside out. The thing about forgiveness that many of us do not realize is that forgiveness is not for the other person, it's for us. Forgiveness allows us to release the pain, hurt and anger so that we can move on. You may need to take some time to discuss the actual process with God to find out the best way to release this person and your resulting emotions. He may ask you to talk to the person, write a letter or pray for them. Sometimes doing these things for someone who hurt you doesn't seem possible in the flesh; this is why it is necessary to seek God's power and guidance. In addition to obtaining freedom in releasing those who have hurt us, remember our discussion from Day 11 of our fast. Mathew tells us that our own forgiveness is dependent upon our ability to forgive others. Think of how often God is hurt by our actions, words and disobedience, but He continues to forgive us over and over again. If God can forgive, who are we not to?

REFLECTIONS: Is there anyone you have not forgiven? List them by name and examine why you have not forgiven them. Then pray and ask God to reveal to you how you can forgive them.

1. _____

_____

2. _____

_____

3. _____

_____

4. _____

_____

Day 33

Daily Prayer: *Lord, help me to understand that everything I do should be for Your glory, help me to recognize when I am not and give me the humility to change, in Jesus' name, Amen.*

Is it for your glory or His-**Daily Scriptures**: 1 Corinthians 10:31

Discussion: Oftentimes we go about our day without realizing that everything we do should be for the glory of God. Think about your daily schedule: Are you consciously living so God will get glory from everything you do? If you are angry, is God receiving glory? If you are overeating, is that bringing glory to God? First Corinthians says whatever we do, do it all for the glory of God. If we can keep in mind that we are living solely to give glory to God, then our behavior, attitude and the decisions we make throughout the day would be much easier. When we find ourselves struggling with sin, ask yourself if the thought, action or response will bring glory to God. This questioning will allow us an opportunity to pause and think about what comes next. Our love for God should compel us to do the right thing and make the right choice to ultimately bring glory to God.

Day 34

Daily Prayer: *Heavenly Father, help me to complete the work You have for me to do. Lord, I need Your direction and guidance to stay on task and finish my assignment, in Jesus' name, Amen.*

Stop procrastinating-**Daily Scriptures**: Genesis 6:8, 12-22

Discussion: What would have happened if Noah decided to hold off on building the ark? God would have had to start all over because no one would have been left. Have you missed out on a particular opportunity because you hesitated or waited too long to take action? You will not know the consequences of your delay until it is too late. In Noah's case, his delay would mean the end of all mankind. Don't miss out on what God has for you as a result of procrastination, fear or laziness. Take advantage of every minute of the day. It is a gift from God, so make the most of it. Tomorrow is not promised.

REFLECTIONS: Have you made any promises you have yet to keep? List them.

1. _____

2. _____

3. _____

Now write the dates you will complete them and put them on your calendar.

1. _____

2. _____

3. _____

Day 35

Daily Prayer: *Thank You, Lord, for Your love and for showing us what it means to love. Strengthen me, Lord, so I have the courage to love like You, in Your Son's name, Amen.*

The love of God-**Daily Scriptures**: 1 John 4:7-21

Discussion: First John 4 describes the love of God. It clearly says to love one another. It does not say love one another until they say or do something to hurt your feelings or upset you; it is not conditional love, it's just love. When you accept Christ into your heart, the Holy Spirit begins to dwell within you. Since the love of God dwells in you, there should be no room for nasty attitudes, selfishness, lying, cheating or anything that is not a characteristic of love. Another attribute of love is that perfect love casts out fear. Fear can be crippling and debilitating to the point where you cannot even move. Recognizing that love can cast out fear can bring you hope and comfort. Many times, you hear excuses as to why things don't get done due to money, situations or circumstances; but more often than not, the bottom line is fear. People often allow fear to hinder them from achieving their hopes and dreams: completing school, starting relationships, staying in relationships or starting a business. It may be a fear of being rejected, a fear of failure or fear of being hurt. Remember, 2 Timothy 1:7 says that God has not given us the spirit of fear. We don't have to allow fear to stop us from anything. The next time you feel fearful, keep in mind that you already have the victory. Even with failure and rejection, we can always take away a lesson learned through that experience. Since all things work for our good, God will turn our disappointments into blessings. It will always work out in our favor. If for no other reason, you will learn what not to do. But even if you are afraid, do it anyway. God is with us; He will never leave us nor forsake us.

Day 36

Daily Prayer: *Heavenly Father, help me to trust You, listen and obey every Word. Lord, be a lamp and a light to make my path clear, in Jesus' name, Amen.*

No guess work-**Daily Scriptures**: Proverbs 6:3-5, 16:3, Jeremiah 29:11, Psalm 37:23

Discussion: Oftentimes in life, we want to make our own way and figure things out on our own. Doing things this way may have a price. Many times, following our own path may cost us precious commodities such as time, money and relationships. One of the benefits to becoming a Christian is that we don't have to figure anything out on our own. Psalm 37:23 says, "The steps of a good man are ordered by the Lord." God already has a route mapped out specifically for every single one of us. We only need to seek Him, trust Him and acknowledge Him in everything we do, and He will direct our paths. Why go through life hitting every pothole and dead-end street when God has all of the up-to-date information on the roadways of our life complete with road closures, detours and weather warnings?

WEEKLY CHALLENGE: Choose your favorite weekly challenge and repeat it for the remainder of the fast.

Day 37

Daily Prayer: *Heavenly Father, I pray that You would guide me so I am able to be obedient to Your every Word and not be swayed but my own flesh or other people or influences, in Jesus' name, Amen.*

Be obedient-Deuteronomy 28, 1 Samuel 15:18-23 (NCV)

Discussion: In Deuteronomy 28, God is explaining the rewards of obedience and the consequences of disobedience. We tend to be rational and analytical people, and we prefer to know how a specific choice or behavior will lead to an expected outcome. God, being our Creator, knows how we think and understand. He wrote this scripture straightforward and completely clear so there would be no possibility of misunderstanding it. Take note that the consequences of disobedience are extremely severe. Why face turmoil and pain when we could simply follow God's lead and reap all the benefits that result from obedience? In 1 Samuel, chapter 15, Samuel is explaining to Saul that obedience is more important to God than making sacrifices. Saul decided to partially obey God. If your boss told you to do tasks A., B. and C. and you only completed A. and B. because you wanted to straighten up the office, although your boss might appreciate the thought, effort and gesture itself, the expectation was for you to complete the tasks you were given. To deviate or disregard instruction is disobedience. As a result of Saul's defiance, God revoked his anointing to be king of Israel. Don't allow disobedience to cause you to lose your anointing, blessings or favor; choose obedience over sacrifice.

Day 38

Daily Prayer: *Dear Lord, help me to always walk with a spirit of love, accept and receive the truth about my sin, and have the courage to hold others accountable, in Jesus' mighty name, Amen.*

Accountability within the Body of Christ-**Daily Scriptures**: 1 Corinthians 5:9-12 (NKJV), Matthew 7:1-5

Discussion: It is common to hear people use Matthew 7:1, "Judge not, that ye not be judged," when confronted about some sin in their lives. To gain the whole picture, it is imperative to continue reading. The scripture goes on to say that before you can help your brother, you must first deal with the sin in your own life. Matthew is saying to correct ourselves before attempting to help our brother, and be sure to approach them from a place of love and not judgment. As a body of believers, we should all be working together to uplift, support and encourage one another. In 1 Corinthians, chapter 5, Paul tells us that within the Body of Christ, we should hold each other accountable if someone is misrepresenting or destroying the witness of Christ, always coming from a genuine place of love and concern, being mindful that we ourselves are not perfect. The man referenced in the story claimed to be a Christian but his lifestyle displayed something other than Christianity. In these types of situations, Paul advises us to love from a distance because "a little leaven leavens the whole lump" (1 Corinthians 5:6). Be careful of the company you keep, being mindful that we are representatives of Jesus Christ our Lord.

REFLECTIONS: Has someone ever called you out about some sin in your life? _____

How did you receive it? Did you feel like they were being judgmental? Were they being judgmental? _____

_____

Are you comfortable enough to hold someone else accountable for their actions? Why or why not? _____

_____

Day 39

Daily Prayer: *Lord, I pray that You would teach me how to be a fisher of men; mold me like You did with Peter, James and John. Show me how to be a disciple for Christ, in Jesus' name I pray, Amen.*

Are you a fisherman-**Daily Scriptures**: Matthew 4:19, Psalm 37:23, Proverbs 16:1-9 (NLT), 1 Thessalonians 5:17, 2 Timothy 2:15 (AMP)

Discussion: As Christians, what should be our ultimate goal? Well, in Matthew, Jesus says that if we follow Him, He will make us fishers of men. Our purpose is to win souls for Christ. God has equipped us with specific gifts and talents to do this. If your goal is something other than using your gifts and talents for winning souls and expanding the Kingdom of God, you may need to rethink what your objectives are as a Christian and seek God for what you should be doing. Like everything in life, there are stages or progressions and there should always be growth. Well, how do we grow in Christ? First Thessalonians says to pray without ceasing. We need an active prayer life. When we spend time with Christ, He can prepare us for things to come. Second Timothy says study to show thyself approved so that we can be presentable to God and fully understand and teach His Word. We wouldn't walk into an operating room and attempt to perform surgery, so why do we go about living life without consulting the Author of life? Don't refuse to turn on the lights and walk around in the dark.

Day 40

Daily Prayer: *Dear Lord, I pray that Your Word will penetrate my heart, and I am able to lead by example as I follow You, in Jesus' name, Amen.*

Lead by example-**Daily Scriptures**: John 13:12-15, 1 Timothy 4:12

Discussion: Being a leader is not always about telling people where to go and what to do. Matthew 23:11 says the greatest among you shall be your servant. In John, Christ made a point to wash the feet of His disciples for us to understand that we have to be willing to serve to be able to lead. You must remain humble and treat others the way you want to be treated. Being a leader is not easy. You must be willing to work. You must be approachable, humble and wise. Strive to be like Christ; He is the ultimate example for us as leaders.

Are you in a position of leadership? _____

Do you lead by example or are you a "do as I say and not as I do" leader? _____

Would the people you lead agree? _____

What can you do to be a better leader? _____

_____

_____

_____

<u>IT IS FINISHED</u>

Congratulations, you have completed your 40-day fast. I commend you for your commitment, your desire to grow your faith, and your spiritual relationship with God. I am certain this was not an easy journey. You may have felt uncomfortable or even encountered spiritual attacks, but you made it. I pray that you will receive everything that God has for you. Thank you for choosing this book to help guide you to being exactly who God called you to be.

BECOMING WHO GOD WANTS YOU TO BE

FASTING is a voluntary abstinence from something deemed as necessary or important. Often times food is restrained from and/or limited for a particular period of time as a religious observance.

Mark 9:29 KJV - And he said unto him, this kind can come forth by nothing, but by prayer and fasting.

Throughout the bible fasting has been used as a tool to focus on a specific request from God.

Nicole L. Crawford shares her experience with fasting and how it may help to strengthen your relationship and evoke the response you desire from God. Using biblicle scripture she describes:

* What is fasting

* How to fast

* The application of fasting to becoming who God wants you to be

Nicole L. Crawford has written and facilitated an annual fast for the last 3 years and was the inspiration for this guide. As an author she has also written screenplays and childrens books. Her love for writing extends to music lyrics s well. Be on the lookout for more from Nicole L. Crawford through Royalty Kingdom Publishing.